VERY THANK YOU !

Your first and last name:

_____

_____

 *Your notes and drawings*

 *Your notes and drawings*

Your notes and drawings

Your notes and drawings

Your notes and drawings

 Your notes and drawings

Your notes and drawings

Your notes and drawings

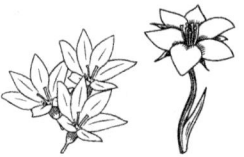

Your notes and drawings

Your notes and drawings

Your notes and drawings

 Your notes and drawings

 *Your notes and drawings*

Your notes and drawings

Your notes and drawings

 Your notes and drawings

Your notes and drawings

 *Your notes and drawings*

Your notes and drawings

Your notes and drawings

Your notes and drawings

 Your notes and drawings

 Your notes and drawings

 *Your notes and drawings*

 Your notes and drawings

Your notes and drawings

Your notes and drawings

Your notes and drawings

Your notes and drawings

Your notes and drawings

Your notes and drawings

Your notes and drawings

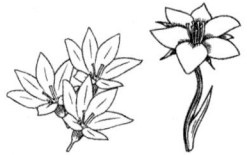

Your notes and drawings

Your notes and drawings

Your notes and drawings

  *Your notes and drawings*

Your notes and drawings

Your notes and drawings

Your notes and drawings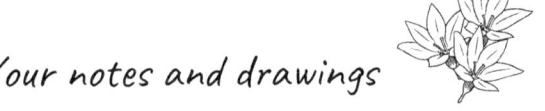

Your notes and drawings

Your notes and drawings

 Your notes and drawings

Your notes and drawings

Your notes and drawings

Your notes and drawings

Your notes and drawings

 Your notes and drawings

 Your notes and drawings

Your notes and drawings

Your notes and drawings

Your notes and drawings

Your notes and drawings

Your notes and drawings

 Your notes and drawings

Your notes and drawings

Your notes and drawings

Your notes and drawings

 Your notes and drawings

Your notes and drawings

 Your notes and drawings

 Your notes and drawings

 *Your notes and drawings*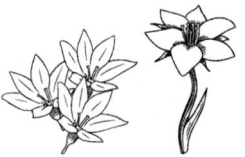

Your notes and drawings

 Your notes and drawings

Your notes and drawings

Your notes and drawings

Your notes and drawings

Your notes and drawings

Your notes and drawings

Your notes and drawings

 *Your notes and drawings*

Your notes and drawings

Your notes and drawings

Your notes and drawings

Your notes and drawings

Your notes and drawings

Your notes and drawings

 Your notes and drawings

Your notes and drawings

Your notes and drawings

 Your notes and drawings

Your notes and drawings

Your notes and drawings

Your notes and drawings

Your notes and drawings

Your notes and drawings

Your notes and drawings

Your notes and drawings

Your notes and drawings

 *Your notes and drawings*

Your notes and drawings

Your notes and drawings

 Your notes and drawings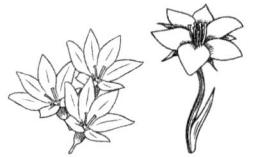

Your notes and drawings

Your notes and drawings

Your notes and drawings

Your notes and drawings

Your notes and drawings

Your notes and drawings

 Your notes and drawings

Your notes and drawings

Your notes and drawings

 Your notes and drawings

 Your notes and drawings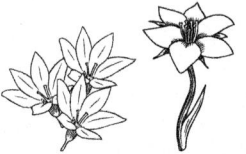

Your notes and drawings

Your notes and drawings

Your notes and drawings

Your notes and drawings

THANK YOU SO MUCH!

Printed in Great Britain
by Amazon